MESSAGE OF WALSINGHAM

based on the original text by
R. W. Connelly SM

*All CTS booklets
are published thanks to the
generous support of its Members*

CATHOLIC TRUTH SOCIETY
PUBLISHERS TO THE HOLY SEE

CONTENTS

INTRODUCTION

It is just over 100 years since Catholic pilgrimages returned to the ancient Shrine of Our Lady of Walsingham. As we celebrate our Centenary much has been achieved and there is much to be thankful for. The Slipper Chapel remains the focus of the National Shrine and in 1981 Cardinal Hume blessed the new Chapel of Reconciliation. Our pilgrim accommodation is at last complete and pilgrims come to Walsingham in ever-increasing numbers to honour the Mother of God and her Son.

Father Connelly's booklet remains an excellent and popular guide to Walsingham and its history. It is my hope that all who read it will be encouraged to come to England's Nazareth - the National Shrine of Our Lady at Walsingham.

Father Alan Williams, SM
Director of the National Shrine
Feast of the Annunciation
25 March 1998

PREFACE

The pilgrim is a seeker. He is searching for God, a deeper understanding of God's goodness and a personal relationship with him. He is always seeking; he will never find his final answer in this world. The true pilgrim is always in transit; he never really arrives.

The Ancient Shrine of Our Lady of Walsingham, England's national shrine, is set in a tiny village on the north coast of East Anglia, not too far from the local capital, Norwich. Its history dates from 1061 and is filled with the spirit of the evangelization of England and the traumas of the Reformation and pilgrims have continued to make their way there for centuries. Paupers and kings have walked, 'slipperless', the last holy mile.

As Fr Connelly says, in Walsingham Mary is contemplated as Mary of Nazareth, the warm hearted Mother of a family that has her Son as the centre. The Christ-centred life of the humble family in Nazareth shows a very human mother engaged in the ordinary household tasks, in poor circumstances but dominated by the presence of God. It is from this well that pilgrims draw water.

Walsingham, we are told, is not a religious oasis surrounded by the bleak desert of the world. Nor is it a place of quiet retreat with the world firmly shut out. It is a vital part of our present world. And it is with this experience of the world that pilgrims tread the path to this Shrine. Pilgrims pray for themselves and they pray for others. Their greatest companion is the Word of God. They come in response to a deep felt call to conversion, to look again at Christ, to turn back to him. They can come in doubt and anxiety to seek guidance for themselves and others; they can come to give blessing, hearts full of gratitude to Christ for his loving care and protection. Pilgrims ask gifts from God.

It is in this light that Walsingham attempts to present Mary to the world, and if the Shrine is true to its traditions then it teaches and witnesses to God's continual presence in each family of the world. It teaches and witnesses to the spirit of Nazareth - the simple spirit of firm faith, ardent trust, fervent prayer and unassuming poverty.

This little booklet has been updated and devotional material has been added. It is hoped that readers and pilgrims will be helped in their journey to and at the Shrine - to meet Our Lord and his Mother. It was Mary herself who said: 'Do all that he tells you'.

HISTORY

Walsingham has been a place of special devotion to Our
Lady since the days of Saxon England, and it is inevitable
that history should play its proper part in an
understanding of the Shrine today. Yet this great and
glorious history does not diminish in any way the
significance of a Shrine which belongs always to the
present age.

Walsingham is for today and the justification for its
continued existence is the role it fulfils in the religious
life of modern man. If it belongs entirely to the past; if it
is cherished merely as a static monument to the piety of
our forebears; if it is seen as a symbol of the good old
days; then it is of little practical value to the People of
God faced with the problems, tensions and needs of the
twentieth century.

An understanding of Walsingham demands an
appreciation of the historical past, but always the
emphasis must be on the present. To be continually
looking back over one's shoulder to the great days gone
by implies the danger of failing to see the opportunities of

the present age and so easily leads to an old-fashioned, out-of-date and irrelevant outlook.

Yet to go to the other extreme and ignore history completely is to shut one's eyes to a rich heritage and refuse the gifts of religious genius and inspiration so carefully garnered over the centuries.

The historian has no exclusive right to Walsingham, but he has a valuable role to play. When dealing with a history that goes back beyond the days of literacy difficulties abound. When documentary evidence is sparse or non-existent, there is always the tendency to enhance the real story by myth and legend. Walsingham has suffered much at the hands of medieval romancers and those who perpetuate such stories today do little service to the Shrine or the Lady they seek to serve. The extraordinary story of Walsingham needs no prop from imagination and in our own scientific age such stories tend to reflect on the credibility of valid history. A proper investigation by those scholars who specialise in the deciphering of myths and legends would serve a valuable purpose in separating undoubted fact from its entangling fiction, but so far little of this work has been attempted.

Origins of Walsingham

Indeed, not very much historical research has been done, and there remain many opportunities for further scholarship. What emerges is a real history which despite the gaps is sufficient to witness to the extraordinary religious popularity of the pre-Reformation Shrine and the extraordinary conquest of man-made difficulties in more recent times.

Walsingham has been a place of pilgrimage since 1061. This is the traditional date and is based upon the statement in the Pynson Ballad published in the last years of the fifteenth century.

In that year, when St Edward the Confessor was King of England, five years before the Norman Conquest, a lady of the village, Richeldis de Faverches, received a vision from Our Lady. The Pynson Ballad relates how Richeldis was 'led in spirit' to the Holy Land and shown the house where Mary was told she was to be the Mother of God. Richeldis was then requested by Our Lady to build another house like this at Walsingham and was promised: 'Whoever seeks my help there will not go away empty-handed'.

This vision is the start of the Walsingham story. It shows that Mary herself selected Walsingham as a holy place, and invited people to visit her and seek her aid.

Richeldis built her house as requested. It was a wooden Saxon house and no attempt was made to imitate Palestinian architecture. Legend has claimed that the Holy House of Walsingham was the real house of Our Lady transported by angels, but the little Saxon house belied any Middle Eastern connections, and this Walsingham legend is the basis for the later and much better known legend of the Holy House of Loreto.

It was a significant sign of the times when few people could read or write and symbols were common that a house should be built to symbolise the house in Nazareth and to remind the faithful of the wonders which had taken place there. It was a later generation which developed this idea into the widespread use of statues, but it is impossible to know when a statue was first introduced into the Holy House.

Growth of Walsingham

The fame of Walsingham as a place of special devotion to Our Lady, and indeed where miracles were said to occur, spread far beyond Norfolk, and pilgrims came from every part of the country.

Henry III would seem to have been the first King of England to visit Walsingham. His visit is recorded in 1226 and he returned several times. Continued royal patronage and frequent visits from almost every King and Queen of England for three hundred years were powerful influences in transforming Walsingham into first a national and then an international shrine.

A Priory of Augustinian Canons was founded in 1153 to see to the spiritual needs of pilgrims. A magnificent Priory Church was built but the simple Holy House remained the centre of devotion.

It is remarkable that no attempt was made to improve the Holy House. It is usual to expect that as shrines become more poplar and revenue increases the original shrine is replaced by a bigger and better one. In Walsingham the original shrine remained untouched. It was merely encased in a stone structure called the Novum Opus so that it was protected from the weather.

As the Shrine and Priory grew so did the village. Hostels were built for pilgrims; trade flourished; the number of residents increased. In the growth of the village Fr Gilbert OFM Cap. has traced a geographical pattern based on Nazareth so that people were continually reminded that this was England's Nazareth.

Walsingham's Stature

It is difficult for us today to realise the importance attached to the Holy Land by the medieval mind. The Crusades show the continual endeavour to rescue the Holy Places from the Saracen and illustrate the longing in every Christian heart to visit the sites of Christ's life on earth. If the pilgrim was prevented from visiting the real Nazareth he could at least visit England's Nazareth as a substitute and this would seem to account for the amazing growth of the Norfolk shrine.

It is not possible to be precise about the vast numbers of pilgrims who visited Walsingham. In an age when pilgrimage was common huge crowds were accepted as normal, just as they are at football matches today. They are not noted for historical reference. It is however certain that the populace followed the king, and in the wake of each king's visit came thousands of his subjects.

There is evidence also of Walsingham's national character from the wills and bequests made in all parts of England. A local shrine was hardly known outside its own locality but Walsingham was known to all England.

Indeed Walsingham was so well known that it is said that at some time in his life every Englishman visited Our Lady of Walsingham, and the Elizabethan chronicler,

Holinshead, gave the road to Walsingham first place among his roads of England.

The four great shrines of medieval Christendom were Jerusalem, Rome, St James of Compostella and Walsingham, and it is significant that the English shrine was the only one dedicated to Mary the Mother of God.

The Reformation

King Henry VIII came to Walsingham in 1511 to give thanks for the birth of his son, Prince Henry. He had a remarkable devotion to Our Lady; maintained the King's priest at the Shrine; permanently endowed the King's candle before the statue. But when he effected his tragic break with Rome, he set in motion the forces which ruthlessly destroyed the grandeur of Walsingham. The Priory was closed; the Canons dispersed on pension; the Holy House burned to the ground; the revered statue transported to London and desecrated.

The Desolation

For over 350 years Walsingham was to be a land of desolation. With the Priory in ruins, the village seemed to forget its religious heritage. The vast majority of

Englishmen had no interest in Our Lady of Walsingham. Even many Catholics through the difficult days of persecution found it difficult to preserve the memory of a shrine they could not visit. Yet it is remarkable that despite all the vicissitudes of English Catholics they never completely forgot the Lady of Walsingham.

By the middle of the nineteenth century, when ideas of religious freedom were once more acceptable, a new interest in Walsingham developed in Catholic circles. Edmund Waterton in his great work Pietas Mariana Britannica (British Devotion to Mary) had a special chapter on Walsingham, but writing in 1879 he was ahead of practical propositions and nothing was effected until 1897.

Charlotte Boyd

In the early 1890s an Anglican lady, Miss Charlotte Boyd, bought the fourteenth century Slipper Chapel at Houghton St Giles. Situated at the final junction of the pilgrim routes as they crossed the ford on the River Stiffkey, it was the last of the old Station Chapels just one mile outside Walsingham. It was in disrepair and had been used for many years as a barn.

In 1894 Miss Boyd made a pilgrimage to all the shrines of Our Lady in Belgium, and while in Bruges attended some of the conferences given by the eminent English Jesuit, Father Clark, in the course of a retreat to the canonesses of St Augustine. At the end of the retreat Miss Boyd left the Church of England and was received into the Catholic Church on 12 September 1894.

As a Catholic, Miss Boyd devoted herself wholeheartedly to the restoration of the Slipper Chapel and it was her intention to make it the Walsingham Shrine. She was a lady with decidedly Benedictine tastes. In her Anglican days she had worked for the restoration of Benedictine monasticism and two of her closest friends were Dom Bede Camm OSB and Dom Philibert Feasey OSB, both ex-Anglicans. As an Oblate of Downside it was to be expected that, having repaired the Slipper Chapel at her own expense, she should offer it to the sons of St Benedict, and Prior Ford of Downside was happy to accept on behalf of his community.

1897: Annus Mirabilis

In 1897 there was not one Catholic living in Walsingham and it formed part of the extensive parish of

King's Lynn. A new parish church was built in King's Lynn and the parish priest, Father Wrigglesworth, incorporated in the design a chapel of Our Lady of Walsingham. Pope Leo XIII expressed an interest in his plans and it is commonly accepted that the Pope blessed the statue. Mr Martin Gillett, who made an intensive study of this period, found no evidence that this actually happened but showed that the statue was carved at Oberammergau and paid for by friends of Father Wrigglesworth.

It was unfortunate that the King's Lynn Shrine was based on the Holy House of Loreto, a shrine 230 years later than the original Shrine at Walsingham. Nevertheless, Our Lady had returned, if not to Walsingham then at least to the parish of which Walsingham formed part, and it was this chapel which was restored by rescript, dated 6 February 1897, of Pope Leo XIII as the Shrine of Our Lady of Walsingham.

MODERN TIMES

The first pilgrimage to Walsingham since the Reformation was made on 20 August 1897. It was a small group of those who attended the opening of the new Church and Shrine in King's Lynn. Led by Father Wrigglesworth, Prior Ford of Downside, and Father Fletcher, the Founder of the Guild of Our Lady of Ransom, they prayed outside the closed Slipper Chapel and visited the site of the ancient Shrine in the village.

It was a small beginning, but it was an important step forward in the restoration of Our Lady of Walsingham.

Slow Development

Hopes for a rapid development of the Slipper Chapel Shrine were sadly misplaced. Attention was paid to the Shrine of Our Lady of Walsingham in King's Lynn, and the Slipper Chapel remained cared for by Downside but unused. Miss Boyd's plans for the return of pilgrims to Walsingham was not fulfilled in her lifetime. She died in obscurity on Tuesday, 3 April 1906, having received the Last Sacraments from her Parish Priest in Kilburn, Father

James O'Reilly, Provincial of the Oblates of Mary Immaculate.

For many years the Slipper Chapel remained an empty church as pilgrims continued to visit King's Lynn. It was not until 1933 that any official steps were taken to implement Miss Boyd's plans for a public shrine. Bishop Laurence Youens was consecrated Bishop of Northampton on 25 July of that year, and announced in the course of the celebrations that it was his firm intention to devote his episcopate to the restoration of devotion to Our Lady in Walsingham.

First National Pilgrimage

The Bishop's enthusiasm for this cause was matched by the enthusiasm of Cardinal Francis Bourne, Archbishop of Westminster, and plans were made for a formal pilgrimage the following year.

In August 1934, Bishop Youens celebrated what was believed to be the first Mass in the Slipper Chapel since the Reformation. On 19 August Cardinal Bourne presided at High Mass in St John's Church, Norwich, and afterwards led a throng of some 12,000 pilgrims to Walsingham, where Benediction was given at an open air altar in the field across the lane from the Slipper Chapel.

It was a significant day. The last Cardinal to visit Walsingham had been Cardinal Wolsey in 1517. He had come as a sick man to pray for his health. Cardinal Bourne also came as a sick man; it was one of his last official engagements; he died the following January and the pulpit in Westminster Cathedral records his gratitude to God for the privilege of restoring pilgrimage to Walsingham.

England's National Shrine

The Slipper Chapel's role as England's National Shrine of Our Lady dates from this year of the first National Pilgrimage. The Chapel was generously donated by the Benedictines of Downside to the Diocese of Northampton and Bishop Youens supported by the English Hierarchy used every endeavour to bring more and more pilgrims to England's ancient shrine.

Years of Progress

The first resident priest was appointed to the Slipper Chapel in 1935. He was Father Bruno Scott-James, a recent convert from the Church of England. At first he lived in the Slipper Chapel Cottage but later removed to Friday Market, to a house which belonged to the Bishop of Northampton. In this house, in an upstairs room, he opened the Chapel of St Aelred which was used by the local Catholics until the Parish Church of the Annunciation was built. This house also served for many years as the headquarters of the Shrine organisation and provided hostel accommodation for many pilgrims.

In 1938 Father Scott-James built a new sacristy, the Chapel of the Holy Ghost adjacent to the Slipper Chapel, and also provided in the Meadow a wooden altar with shelter, so that the large crowds of pilgrims who now flocked to Walsingham could hear Mass even in inclement weather.

In that same year of 1938 Cardinal Hinsley led a huge pilgrimage of youth to pray for peace and on 8 September the Slipper Chapel was re-consecrated.

American Devotion

During the 1939-45 War Walsingham saw an inevitable decrease in the numbers of civilian pilgrims but the presence of many American servicemen in East Anglia served to introduce Our Lady of Walsingham to the

United States, and it was the American Air Force which was privileged to arrange the first Mass since the Reformation on the site of the high altar in the ruins of the old Priory Church.

Today there is an American Shrine to Our Lady of Walsingham, at Williamsburg, Virginia.

Anglican Devotion

In the intervening years between the first pilgrimage of 1897 and the National Pilgrimage of 1934 there had been a great resurgence of devotion to Our Lady among certain members of the Church of England. The Vicar of Walsingham, Father A. Hope Patten had a particular and touching devotion to Our Lady of Walsingham, and in the early 1920s led his parish in an ardent attempt to develop this devotion within the Church of England. In 1934 he built in the village a magnificent Shrine Church which continues to attract many thousands of devout Anglican pilgrims each year. This church is now in the care of a College of Guardians, and Father Hope Patten's great work has been continued by his successors.

Ecumenism

The existence of two Shrines of Our Lady so close to each other inevitably causes some wonder, but the facts of historical separation cannot be lightly ignored. Separate Shrines as indeed separate Churches will always be an anomaly, but the true work of ecumenism is to accept the pain of the present separation whilst using every endeavour to effect a new understanding and unity. Relations between the two Shrines are close and cordial, based on a mutual respect and realisation that both are working for the same end: to worship God by honouring his Mother.

Joint pilgrimages are often held and pilgrims from each tradition visit both Shrines to pray together in warm Christian fellowship that Our Lady, who seemed such a source of discord at the time of the Reformation, may now become more and more a unifying influence for her Son's Church in the world today.

Slipper Chapel Statue

All Catholic pilgrimage devotions are centred on the Slipper Chapel, where the statue of Our Lady of Walsingham is enthroned. The statue is of course a modern one but has been modelled as closely as possible on the medieval statue. Our Lady is depicted in traditional style seated on a simple chair of state with the Child on her knee. She wears a Saxon crown in token of her ancient queenship and carries the lily of purity.

The statue is not remarkable in itself but the sincere attempt to recreate the form of the old statue when the only available evidence came from the circular pilgrim medallions is praiseworthy and the result is pleasing and devotional.

It is a thought-provoking statue with theological implications so typical of the Middle Ages. The Child seems to dominate. It is not so much a statue of the Mother with the Child as a statue of the Child with his Mother in the background. The Child holds the Book of Gospels with one hand and with the other seems to shield his Mother from attack.

In recent years Our Lady has been depicted frequently as a lonely young girl. Our Lady of Lourdes and Our Lady of Fatima stand alone. Our Lady of Walsingham emphasises her Motherhood and her continual effort to present her Son to the world.

The statue has an importance of its own not only because of its situation at the heart of the National Shrine, but because it is one of the few statues in the world to be crowned in the name of the Pope. This was done in Marian Year, on 15 August 1954, by Archbishop O'Hara, who was to become Apostolic Delegate to Great Britain. At the same time the women of England presented a costly crown of gold and jewels which is placed on the statue at certain times.

The devotion to Our Lady of Walsingham received a further mark of papal approval during the visit to Britain of Pope John Paul II in 1982. The statue was taken from the Slipper Chapel to Wembley Stadium and occupied a place of honour on the altar while the Pople celebrated Mass in the presence of many thousands of people.

Site of the Original Shrine

The archaeological excavations undertaken by Mr Charles Green and Mr. A.B. Whittingham in 1961 have proved the authenticity of the traditional view about the site of the old shrine. It is but a lonely stretch of lawn under the shadow of the ruins of the Priory arch. Of the Holy House, nothing remains to be seen except a small wooden plaque set into the ground. Pilgrims can still visit this revered spot like many thousands before them.

There has been some discussion in recent years as to whether the present Shrine should be sited in the Slipper Chapel, which after all is one mile outside Walsingham. At one time it was understood that this was merely a temporary site and that eventually the Shrine would return to Walsingham.

Perhaps in the distant future it will be possible for the Shrine to return to the village, but for the moment it is accepted that there are no practical possibilities for this. The cost of a new shrine would be prohibitive; the provision of land impossible. The old Catholic dream of rebuilding on the ancient site remains a dream. The Priory is in private hands and the owner has no wish to sell his family home.

It may be that future generations will have the privilege of restoring Our Lady to her old home, but in the meantime development will continue at the Slipper Chapel. It will not be in vain. No matter what the future may hold, the Slipper Chapel will always be a place for pilgrims to congregate either as the centre of the Shrine or as the starting point for processions into Walsingham.

PILGRIMS

The pilgrim is a seeker. He is searching for God, a deeper understanding of God's goodness and a closer personal relationship with him. He is always seeking; he will never find his final answer in this world. The true pilgrim is always in transit; he never really arrives.

Pilgrims have always been distinguished by the happy camaraderie of the road. They enjoy the support and company of each other, as well as the generous welcome and hospitality of those they meet on the way. Pilgrimage is not a dull affair as Chaucer's Canterbury pilgrims show so clearly. It is a happy adventure and a joyful experience. The pilgrim grows in love of his fellow men and his characteristic virtue is charity.

There is always some penance in pilgrimage. The hardships of the road are not lightly endured, and in some countries great emphasis has been placed on bare-foot walks, long fasts and sleepless nights. Penance is important and is indeed inevitable whenever a long journey is undertaken, but the traditional English pilgrim has given a greater prominence to charity.

Today's pilgrims to Walsingham are seeking God through Our Lady, and they maintain all the characteristics of the pilgrim of old. Each year, University students from all over the country walk to Walsingham carrying heavy wooden crosses. Each year, a group of men from the Guild of Our Lady of Ransom tramp the old Pilgrim Way from London. Young people walk the twenty-seven miles along a new Pilgrim Way from Our Lady's Chapel on the Red Mount in King's Lynn. Walkers, cyclists and hitch-hikers arrive at the Shrine throughout the summer.

Adventure is the privilege of the youthful pilgrim, but those older people who journey to Walsingham by car and coach do not thereby lose their character of pilgrim. They make their journey with all the discomforts of travelling and they have every opportunity of experiencing the charity of the road.

The pilgrims of today are not old-fashioned men and women living in the past. They are people from every age group aware of the problems of the day and anxious to seek their answers at Our Lady's Shrine.

Pilgrimage Devotions

Walsingham is a place of prayer. The pilgrim comes to pray. There is a unique religious atmosphere recognisable by all, even those who find difficulty in belief. There is opportunity for private meditative prayer; but when larger crowds gather then community and liturgical prayer have an importance all their own.

The Mass is the centre of every pilgrimage, but because space in the Slipper Chapel is limited the Chapel of Reconciliation has been built for larger congregations. In this Chapel the altar has been so placed that it is fully visible from all parts of the outside Meadow, and, when required, specially designed doors are opened and pilgrims in the open air participate in the Mass as intimately as those inside.

This altar, of polished Aberdeen granite, is the gift of the Union of Catholic Mothers and contains authenticated relics of St Thomas More, St Thomas of Canterbury and St Lawrence the Martyr.

The theme of reconciliation is emphasised within the Chapel, where there is ample provision for the celebration of the Sacrament of Reconciliation.

Mary plays her proper part in liturgical life as well as in community life and individual devotions. Her statue is carried along the processional route from the village. In the Slipper Chapel, candles and flowers demonstrate the love and affection of pilgrims. The Rosary and Litany of Walsingham are recited frequently by pilgrims begging her to join her prayers to theirs.

Yet Walsingham attempts no stereotyped devotion. There is a basic plan for community devotion, but each pilgrim is an individual with individuals tastes and interests, and the freedom of the children of God demands that each be free to express a personal love in his or her own way.

DEVOTIONS FOR PILGRIMAGE

Departure for a safe Pilgrimage

Let us pray. Heavenly Father, who made the Sons of Israel to walk with dry feet through the midst of the sea, and who did open to the Three Wise Men, by the guiding of a Star, the way that led to you.

Grant to us we beseech you, a safe journey and a time of tranquiltiy, that accompanied by your Holy Angel, we may arrive safely in Walsingham, and on return to our homes.

We ask this through Christ Our Lord. Amen.

During the Journey and on the Holy Mile

The Mysteries of the Rosary

The Joyful Mysteries
1. The Annunciation
2. Mary's visit to Elizabeth
3. The Birth of Jesus Christ

4.   The Presentation in the Temple
5.   The finding of the Child Jesus in the Temple

The Sorrowful Mysteries
1.   The Agony in the Garden of Gethsemane
2.   The Scourging of the Lord
3.   The Mocking and Crowning with Thorns
4.   The Carrying of the Cross
5.   The Crucifixion

The Glorious Mysteries
1.   The Resurrection of Christ
2.   The Ascension of Christ into Heaven
3.   The Coming of the Holy Spirit at Pentecost
4.   The Assumption of Our Lady
5.   The Crowning of Our Lady in Heaven.

Hail, holy Queen, mother of mercy; hail, our life, our sweetness, and our hope! To thee do we cry, poor banished children of Eve; to thee do we send up our sighs, mourning and weeping in this vale of tears. Turn then, most gracious advocate, thine eyes of mercy towards us; and after this our exile, show unto us the blessed fruit of thy womb, Jesus.

O clement, O loving, O sweet Virgin Mary.

Pray for us, O holy Mother of God.

That we may be made worthy of the promises of Christ.

Let us pray: O God, whose only-begotten Son, by his life, death and resurrection, has purchased for us the rewards of eternal life, grant, we beseech thee, that meditating on these mysteries, in the most holy Rosary of the Blessed Virgin Mary, we may both imitate what they contain, and obtain what they promise, through the same Christ our Lord. Amen.

The Angelus

The Angel of the Lord declared unto Mary,
And she conceived of the holy Spirit.
Hail Mary ...
Behold the handmaid of the Lord,
Be it done to me according to thy word.
Hail Mary ...
And the Word was made flesh
And dwelt among us.
Hail Mary ...
Pray for us, O Holy Mother of God.
That we may be made worthy of the promises
of Christ.

Let us Pray: Pour forth, we beseech you, O Lord, your grace into our hearts, that we, to whom the incarnation of Christ your Son was made known by the message of an angel, may by his passion and cross, be brought to the glory of his resurrection, through the same Christ our Lord. Amen.

May the divine assistance remain always with us and may the souls of the faithful departed, through the mercy of God, rest in peace, Amen.

Visit to the Holy Ghost Chapel

Prayer to the Holy Spirit:

'I am going to reveal to you a Secret of Sanctity and Happiness: if every day, during five minutes, you will keep your imagination quiet, shut your eyes to all the things of sense, and close your ears to all the sounds of earth, in order to be able to withdraw into the Sanctuary of your Baptised Soul, which is the Temple of the Holy Spirit, speaking there to that Holy Spirit, saying:

'Holy Spirit, soul of my soul I adore thee; enlighten, guide, strengthen and console me; tell me what I ought to do and command me to do it, I promise to be submissive in everything that You shall ask of me and to accept all that You permit to happen to me, only show me what is Your will'.

If you do this, your life will pass happily and serenely,

consolation will abound even in the midst of troubles, for Grace will be given in proportion to the trial as well as Strength to bear it, bringing you to the Gates of Paradise full of merit, this submission to the Holy Spirit is the Secret of Sanctity'.Cardinal Mercier (1851-1926)

Come Holy Spirit, fill the hearts of your faithful and kindle in them the fire of your love. Send forth your Spirit and they shall be created. And you will renew the face of the earth.

Visit to the Slipper Chapel - the National Shrine of Our Lady

Prayer of Erasmus

O, alone of all women, Mother and Virgin, Mother most blessed, Virgin most pure, we salute you, we honour you as best we can with our humble offerings. May your Son grant us that imitating your most holy manners, we also, by the Grace of the Holy Spirit may deserve to conceive the Lord Jesus spiritually in our inmost soul, and once conceived, never to lose Him. Amen.

Our Lady of Walsingham, pray for us.

The Memorare

Remember, O most loving Virgin Mary, that never was it known that anyone who fled to your protection, implored your help, or sought your intercession, was left unaided. Inspired with this confidence I fly to you, O Virgin of virgins, my Mother. To you do I come, before you I stand, sinful and sorrowful. Mother of the Word Incarnate, despise not my petitions, but in your mercy hear and answer me. Amen.

Prayer for England

O Blessed Virgin Mary, Mother of God and our most gentle Queen and Mother look down in mercy upon England, thy Dowry and upon us all who greatly hope and trust in thee. By thee it was that Jesus, Our Saviour and our hope, was given unto the world; and he has given thee to us that we might hope still more. Plead for us thy children, whom thou didst receive and accept at the foot of the cross, O sorrowful Mother. Intercede for our separated brethren, that with us in the one true fold, they may be united to the Chief Shepherd, the Vicar of thy Son. Pray for us all, dear Mother, that by faith, fruitful in good works we may all deserve to see and praise God, together with you in our heavenly home. Amen.

Prayer for Unity

Father, may they be one. May they be so completely one that the world will realise that it was you who sent me and that I have loved them as much as you loved me.

Visit to the Chapel of Reconciliation

Prayer before Mass

O God, to whom every heart is open, every desire known and from whom no secrets are hidden; purify the thoughts of our hearts by the inspiration of your Holy Spirit, that we may perfectly love you, and worthily praise your holy name. Amen.

Reading from the Gospel according to Luke

The angel Gabriel was sent by God to a town in Galilee called Nazareth, to a virgin betrothed to a man named Joseph, of the House of David, and the virgin's name was Mary. He went in and said to her, 'Rejoice, so highly favoured! The Lord is with you'. She was deeply disturbed by these words and asked herself what this greeting could mean, but the angel said to her, 'Mary, do not be afraid: you have won God's favour. Listen! You are to conceive and bear a son, and you must name him

Jesus. He will be Great and will be called Son of the Most High. The Lord God will give him the throne of his ancestor David: he will rule over the House of Jacob for ever and his reign will have no end.'

This is the Gospel of the Lord.

Praise to you, Lord Jesus Christ.

Litany of Our Lady of Walsingham

Mary, pray to the Lord for us.

Mary, without sin, pray to the Lord for us.

Mary God's Mother, pray to the Lord for us.

Mary the Virgin, pray to the Lord for us.

Mary taken to Heaven, pray to the Lord for us.

Mary at Bethlehem, pray for all mothers.

Mary at Nazareth, pray for all families.

Mary at Cana, pray for all married couples.

Mary at the Cross, pray for all who suffer.

Mary in the Upper Room, pray for all who wait.

Mary model of Womanhood,

pray for all women.

Woman of Faith, keep us in mind.

Woman of Hope, keep us in mind.

Woman of Charity, keep us in mind.

Woman of Suffering, keep us in mind.

Woman of Anxiety, keep us in mind.

Woman of Humility, keep us in mind.

Woman of Poverty, keep us in mind.

Woman of Purity, keep us in mind.

Woman of Obedience, keep us in mind.

Woman who wondered, remember us to God.

Woman who listened, remember us to God.

Woman who followed Him, remember us to God.

Woman who longed for Him, remember us to God.

Woman who loves Him, remember us to God.

Mother of God, be our Mother always.

Mother of Men, be our Mother always.

Mother of the Church, be our Mother always.

Mother of the World, be our Mother always.

Mother we need, be our Mother always.

Mother who went on believing, we thank God for you.

Mother who never lost hope, we thank God for you.

Mother who loved to the end, we thank God for you.

All holy and ever-living God, in giving us Jesus Christ to be our Saviour and Brother, you gave us Mary, His Mother, to be our Mother also; grant us we pray you, to live lives worthy of so great a Brother and so dear a Mother. May we come at last to you the Father of us all, through Jesus Christ your Son, who lives and reigns with you and the Holy Spirit for ever and ever. Amen.

Commendation

Jesus, Mary and Joseph,
I give you my heart and soul.
Jesus, Mary and Joseph,
assist me in my last agony.
Jesus, Mary and Joseph, may I breathe forth my soul in peace with you.
Our Lady of Walsingham, pray for us.

Closing Prayer

Let us pray: Father, give your people the joy of continual health in mind and body. With the prayers of the Virgin Mary to help us, guide us through this life to eternal happiness in the life to come.

We ask this through Christ our Lord. Amen.

MESSAGE OF WALSINGHAM

Understanding Our Lady

All devotion is based on proper understanding of Our Lady's role. She is the Mother of God and we honour her for that reason. Without her Son, she is just one of us; with her Son, she is, after him, the most important human creature of all time.

As the Mother of Jesus, she shared his love as only a mother can; she gave him human life that he might save the world; she interested herself in every detail of his mission; she followed him in suffering to the very foot of the Cross.

It is the bond of love uniting Mother to Son and Son to Mother which is the basis of Catholic devotion. Because Christ, who is God, loves his Mother in this special way, he listens readily to her prayer and accords to her an extraordinary power of intercession. Because Mary loves her Son as Man and God, her love includes an unusual affection for God's children on earth. She ardently desires to use her power of intercession and to further Christ's mission on earth; the salvation and happiness of all men.

Mary is an enigma. On the one hand so close to God; on the other hand so ordinary and human. It is so easy to exaggerate her role until she seems to be indistinguishable from God himself; it is also easy to minimise her role so that she appears to be an ordinary woman indistinguishable from the rest of the human race. To exaggerate or to minimise is not to do justice.

The heart of the matter is Mary's relationship with God. As long as she is seen as the 'Christ-bearer', the Mother of God, then she will be seen in her true perspective.

Mary of Nazareth

In Walsingham, Mary has always been contemplated as Mary of Nazareth, the warm-hearted Mother of a family which has her Son at the centre.

The story of the Annunciation shows her important role in salvation as with utter candour and simplicity she accepts the invitation to be Mother of God. The Christ-centred life of the humble family in Nazareth shows a very human mother engaged in the ordinary household tasks, in poor circumstances but dominated by the presence of God.

It is in this light that Walsingham attempts to present Mary to the world, and if the Shrine is true to its traditions then it teaches and witnesses to God's continual presence in each family of the world. It teaches and witnesses to the spirit of Nazareth - the simple spirit of firm faith, ardent trust, fervent prayer and unassuming poverty.

The Word of God

The pilgrim's search for God is always a personal affair but it entails study and understanding of Holy Scripture. No pilgrim can escape from the vital necessity of learning more about God's love from God's written word.

Devotion to Mary is traditional but is based on Scripture, and as the Church puts greater and greater emphasis on the value of biblical study the role of a Marian Shrine becomes increasingly scriptural.

Each generation has contributed its own genius and insights to the development of devotion to Mary and it may well be that the particular contribution of this generation is to be found in a deepening scriptural theology of Mary's role in salvation.

Great ambitions are foreign to the simplicity of England's Nazareth but there are those who see the Shrine today as a centre of theological study, where theologians can gather for valid discussion and enquiry into 'The Role of the Blessed Virgin Mary, Mother of God, in the Mystery of Christ and the Church'.

In these circumstances the teaching role of the Shrine has been accepted, and conferences and retreats are a regular feature of the Walsingham programme. The homily also has been given greater prominence and Scripture reading becomes an integral part of each pilgrimage.

What do Pilgrims Seek?

There is an element of petition in each pilgrimage. Pilgrims pray for themselves and they pray for others. Often they ask for specific gifts, sometimes material, sometimes spiritual. All requests show a dependence on God; did not Our Lady of Walsingham ask that men should seek her aid?

There is a touching simplicity about the petitions of many pilgrims as they seek help with the trivialities of life. Others, men and women of faith and courage come to seek greater benefits, extraordinary spiritual gifts, even miracles of healing. They come in doubt and anxiety to seek guidance for themselves and others. They come to bring the problems of the world to God.

Walsingham Today

Walsingham is not a religious oasis surrounded by the bleak desert of the world. It is not a place of quiet retreat with the world firmly shut out. It is a vital part of our present world. The agonising cries of God's poor resound in the prayerful silence of the Shrine. The hungry people of the world, the persecuted, the suffering, the sick, the evil people of the world are all present in spirit, and their needs can never be forgotten.

Perhaps never before has the world needed prayer so much; perhaps never before has the world needed Our Lady so much; perhaps never before has the world needed dedicated Christians so much.

The concern of Our Lady for the troubles of the world has been demonstrated by her authentic appearances in so many places in recent times. She does not speak different languages in Lourdes and Fatima and it is the same Lady who speaks from Walsingham.

She is indeed the Mother of Concern, vitally concerned in the success of her Son's mission; vitally concerned about its apparent failure; vitally concerned about the unhappiness and evil of God's children today; vitally concerned that men of good will should join with her to labour for God's kingdom.

What the world needs at this present moment are focal points where men and women can gather to increase their own love for God and so rededicate themselves to God's work for others. Without such renewal and enthusiasm the world will remain as it is.

Walsingham is just such a place of dedication prepared for us by over nine hundred years of devotion. It is established as a place of prayer and a national centre for those who love Our Lady.

It is a place where ordinary men and women can learn that dedication which will send them out with faith, courage and enthusiasm to take God's saving message to their own people and to those who sit in the power of darkness.

Hospitality

The pilgrims arrive in Walsingham as small communities to form the larger community at the Shrine itself. The charity of the road merges into the hospitality of the Shrine. At the Slipper Chapel, the Pilgrim Centre opened in 1970 provides all the amenities to refresh tired and sometimes exhausted pilgrims.

In the village, meals and accommodation are available for those who wish to stay for longer periods. Much has been done in recent years to improve the standards of pilgrim accommodation and the Shrine authorities have built at Elmham House in Friday Market a new wing of modern single rooms with spacious dining room and full kitchen facilities.

In 1986 an additional building was erected to afford proper hospitality for those who are sick or handicapped. Situated at the heart of pilgrim activities in Friday Market, this building has been specially designed to ensure the comfort and convenience of these important pilgrims, who in their sufferings are so close to Our Lady.

Such buildings of course require people to serve those who use them. The permanent community of the Shrine is made up of Marist Fathers and Sisters, a deacon and a dedicated group of lay staff who organise the pilgrimages and the religious services and look after the well-being, material and spiritual, of pilgrims and visitors.

Walsingham Association

In all this work, members of the Walsingham Association play a prominent and valuable role. Founded in 1933 to help with the development of the Shrine and to make Our Lady of Walsingham better known, the Association flourishes with many branches throughout the country.

CTS
MEMBERSHIP

We hope you have enjoyed reading this booklet. If you would like to read more of our booklets or find out more about CTS - why not do one of the following?

1. Join our Readers CLUB.
We will send you a copy of every new booklet we publish, through the post to your address. You'll get 20% off the price too.

2. Support our work and Mission.
Become a CTS Member. Every penny you give will help spread the faith throughout the world. What's more, you'll be entitled to special offers exclusive to CTS Members.

3. Ask for our Information Pack.
Become part of the CTS Parish Network by selling CTS publications in your own parish.

Call us now on 020 7640 0042 or return this form to us at CTS, 40-46 Harleyford Road, London SE11 5AY
Fax: 020 7640 0046 email: info@cts-online.org.uk

❏ I would like to join the *CTS Readers Club*

❏ Please send me details of how to join CTS as a *Member*

❏ Please send me a *CTS Information Pack*

Name:..

Address: ....

....

Post Code:..

Phone: ....

email address: ....

Registered charity no. 218951.
Registered in England as a company limited by guarantee no.57374.